low carb italian

30 DELICIOUS, GUILT FREE
LOW CARB ITALIAN RECIPES
FOR EXTREME WEIGHT LOSS

Published by The Fruitful Mind

www.fruitfulbooks.com

Disclaimer

Table Of Contents

3

Introduction

There are any images that come to mind when we think of Italian cooking. For some it is the picture of a slightly older Italian woman, happily crafting masterpieces that have been in the family for generations. She is content knowing that her food provides love, nourishment and, let's be honest, plenty of carbohydrates to stick to the bones. Or, your image of Italian cuisine may be based on geographical and cultural conditions, such as the light delicious seafood that is abundant along the coast, or the savory cross cultural favorites of the more southern regions. Whatever your picture of the food of Italy is, there is no question that it is one of the most popular and well loved cuisines of the world.

When we merge the tastes of Italy's history with modern diet considerations, it seems as though we reach a point of conflict.

We love the rich, savory flavors however; our diets and our health require that we be more aware and careful of what we put into our bodies. For many of us, this means that the heavy pastas, sauces and cheeses so popular in Italian cuisine are no longer an option. If this is how you have been feeling about your Italian favorites, then there is good news for you. You do not have to sacrifice Italian flavors and textures in order to maintain you low carb lifestyle. Many traditional Italian dishes are naturally low in carbohydrates, even though this goes against our natural perception of the traditional cuisine. Along with this, there are many adaptations that can be made to recreate you carb laden favorites and to breathe new life into dishes you thought were no longer an option in your healthy lifestyle.

This new take on Italian cuisine focuses on flavor and freshness. You will find fresh, natural ingredients used in the recipes contained within this book. Most of them represent what you know as the flavors or Italy, while you will also be surprised by the introduction of new flavors as well. You will notice ingredients such as fresh basil and fresh mozzarella used throughout. There is a reason that the focus is on the freshest and best quality ingredients that you can afford within your budget. The reason is that Italian cuisine is as much about the experience as it is about the nourishment. The difference between fresh robust basil and the dried herb is incredible, and fresh mozzarella melts so smoothly and has a softer, nuttier flavor than its counterparts that you will find packaged in bags and tightly sealed containers. Allow yourself to experience Italian dishes with the new life and vibrancy that only the freshest of ingredients will bring.

The recipes in this book were created with your special dietary considerations in mind. All recipes contain twenty grams or fewer of net carbohydrates. Many of these dishes are calorie and fat conscious as well, however there are richer dishes included in this collection as well. If you encounter a dish that you need to make lighter for your individual dietary needs, you may substitute any richer ingredient for a lighter one, such as low fat cheese for the full fat variety or substituting red wine vinegar for the actual wine listed in the recipe. Taste each recipe as you go and make adjustments as need be.

Embrace your inner Italian chef, and once again embrace the full bounty of flavors from Italy.

Appetizers and Light Bites

Whether you are searching for a refreshing, low carb first course, or a light meal that is full of flavor without feeling heavy, these low fuss nibbles are the perfect answer. Each highlights the freshness of authentic Italian flavors, while being incredibly simple in preparation. Ideal for sharing, or keeping all to yourself.

Roasted Deconstructed Caprese

Prep Time: 5 minutes

Cook Time: 15 minutes

Servings: 4-6

Calories: 136

Fat: 9g

Protein: 5g

Net carbs: 6g

Ingredients:

8 Roma tomatoes, sliced in half lengthwise

2 tablespoons olive oil

2 tablespoons balsamic vinegar

2 cloves garlic, crushed and minced

½ cup fresh mozzarella

2 tablespoons basil, chopped

1 teaspoon fresh ground black pepper

Directions:

Preheat oven to 400 degrees Fahrenheit.

Place tomato slices on the baking sheet.

In a small bowl combine the olive oil, vinegar and garlic. Whisk well and brush over the tomatoes.

Top with fresh mozzarella, basil and black pepper.

Place in the oven and bake for 12-15 minutes.

Serve warm.

Zucchini Boat Bruschetta

Prep Time: 10 minutes

Cook Time: 25 minutes

Servings: 4

Calories: 84

Fat: 4g

Protein: 2g

Net carbs: 9g

Ingredients:

4 large zucchini, cut in half lengthwise

1 tablespoon olive oil

2 tablespoons balsamic vinegar

4 cloves garlic, crushed and minced

1 teaspoon rosemary

1 ½ cup tomatoes, diced

½ cup red onion, diced

1 teaspoon salt

1 teaspoon pepper

Directions:

Preheat oven to 375 degrees Fahrenheit.

Take each zucchini half and hollow out a shallow well along the length of each.

Place on a baking sheet.

Combine olive oil, balsamic vinegar, garlic and rosemary in a small bowl. Whisk well, and brush liberally over the zucchini halves.

Place in the oven and bake for 25-30 minutes.

Remove from oven and let cool slightly.

Top with diced tomatoes, onions, salt and pepper.

Serve warm.

Shrimp and Tomato Appetizer

Prep Time: 10 minutes + 2hours chilling time

Cook Time: 0

Servings: 6-8

Calories: 107

Fat: 3g

Protein: 16g

Net carbs: 3g

Ingredients:

24 medium shrimp, cleaned and cooked

½ cup tomatoes, diced

½ cup red onion, diced

½ cup yellow bell pepper, diced

1 tablespoon olive oil

½ teaspoon salt

1 teaspoon cracked black pepper

1 tablespoon balsamic vinegar

4 cloves garlic, crushed and minced

½ cup fresh basil, chopped

8 endive leaves

Directions:

In a large bowl, combine the shrimp, tomatoes, red onion and bell pepper. Drizzle with olive oil and season with salt, black pepper, balsamic vinegar and garlic. Toss to coat well.

Place in the refrigerator and let chill for
two hours.

Place three shrimp on each endive leave
and garnish with fresh basil.

Serves as an appetizer course or a light
lunch with a salad.

Buttered Garlic Calamari

Prep Time: 10 minutes

Cook Time: 10 minutes

Servings: 4

Calories: 374

Fat: 28g

Protein: 20g

Net carbs: 5g

Ingredients:

1 lb. squid, cut into rings approximately ½ inch thick

½ cup butter

2 teaspoons olive oil

3 cloves garlic, crushed and minced

2 tablespoons shallots, sliced

½ cup dry white wine

¼ fresh grated parmesan cheese

2 tablespoons fresh basil, chopped

1 teaspoon salt

1 teaspoon pepper

Directions:

In a sauté pan over medium heat, add the olive oil, garlic and shallots. Sauté until just tender, about 2-3 minutes.

Add the butter and let it melt, but not brown, before adding the calamari.

Reduce heat to medium low and cook calamari, while tossing, for 4-5 minutes.

Add the white wine and continue cooking until reduced, approximately 3 minutes. Remove from heat and season with parmesan cheese, basil, salt and pepper. Serve as an appetizer or as a topping for a fresh green salad.

Gazpacho Appetizer Shots

Prep Time: 10 minutes+2 hours for chilling

Cook Time: 0

Servings: 4

Calories: 48

Fat: 4g

Protein: 1g

Net carbs: 3g

Ingredients:

1 cup tomatoes, chopped

¼ cup red onion, diced

¼ cup yellow bell pepper, dice

½ cup cucumber, chopped

¼ cup tomato juice

1 tablespoon olive oil

2 teaspoons white wine vinegar

1 teaspoon oregano

1 teaspoon basil

1 teaspoon crushed red pepper flakes

½ teaspoon salt, or more to taste

Lemon slices, for garnish

Celery, cut into two inch pieces, for garnish

Large green olives, for garnish

Directions:

In a bowl combine the tomatoes, red onion, bell pepper and cucumber. Toss well.

Add tomato juice, olive oil and vinegar. Season with oregano, basil, crushed red pepper and salt to taste.

Cover and place in the refrigerator for 2 hours.

Pour into small serving glasses, garnished with a lemon slice and celery and olive skewered with a tooth pick.

Herb, Garlic and White Bean Dip

Prep Time: 10 minutes+2hours chilling

Cook Time: 0

Servings: 4-6

Calories: 177

Fat: 7g

Protein: 7g

Net carbs: 17g

Ingredients:

1 15 ounce can white beans, drained and rinsed

2 tablespoons olive oil

4 cloves garlic, crushed and minced

1 tablespoon fresh rosemary

1 teaspoon tarragon

2 tablespoons fresh lemon juice

1 tablespoon lemon zest

½ teaspoon salt

1 teaspoon pepper

Directions:

Place all ingredients in a food processor and blend until smooth.

Place in a bowl, cover and refrigerate for two hours.

Serve with fresh vegetables and low carb cracker options.

Portabella Mushroom Sandwiches

Prep Time: 10 minutes

Cook Time: 20 minutes

Servings: 4

Calories: 205

Fat: 13g

Protein: 14g

Net carbs: 7g

Ingredients:

8 large Portobello mushroom caps, cleaned

1 tablespoon olive oil

4 cups fresh spinach

1 cup fresh asparagus spears

½ red onion, sliced thinly

2 cloves garlic, crushed and minced

2 Roma tomatoes, sliced

1 cup fresh mozzarella cheese, sliced

¼ cup walnuts, chopped

¼ cup fresh basil

½ teaspoon salt

1 teaspoon pepper

Directions:

Preheat oven to 400 degrees Fahrenheit. Place the mushroom caps on a baking sheet and brush with olive oil. Place in the oven and roast for 10-15 minutes until firm tender.

Meanwhile, in a sauté pan heat the olive oil over medium heat. Add the asparagus and sauté for 2 minutes.

Add the spinach, garlic and red onion. Sauté until spinach is wilted, approximately 2 minutes. Remove from heat and set aside.

Remove mushroom caps from the oven. Top 4 of them with heaping portions of the spinach vegetable mixture, sliced tomato, fresh mozzarella, walnuts, basil leaves and season with salt and pepper.

Place an additional mushroom cap on top of each. Serve warm.

Soups and Salads

Soups and salads make tantalizing first courses, or a delicious meal all on their own. While probably the least carb laden of traditional Italian courses, there is typically still plenty of use of pasta and starchy vegetables to enhance the flavor and textures of these dishes. In these versions, that aspect has been eliminated and replaced with flavor so fresh and explosive that you will never miss the heavier carbohydrate load.

Italian Wedding Soup

Prep Time: 15 minutes

Cook Time: 1 hour

Servings: 6

Calories: 345

Fat: 20g

Protein: 23g

Net carbs: 12g

Ingredients:

Meatballs

1 lb. ground beef

1 egg, beaten

¼ cup fresh grated parmesan cheese

2 cloves garlic, crushed and minced

¼ cup fresh basil, chopped

¼ cup fresh parsley, chopped

1 teaspoon oregano

½ teaspoon crushed red pepper flakes

1 teaspoon salt

1 teaspoon pepper

Soup

6 cups chicken or beef stock

¼ cup dry red wine

4 cups fresh spinach, torn

1 cup red onion, diced

1 cup carrots, diced

1 tablespoon lemon juice

2 bay leaves

1 sprig fresh rosemary

Directions:

Preheat oven to 350 degrees Fahrenheit. In a large bowl combine all of the ingredients for the meatballs. Using your hands, mix well to make sure all ingredients are evenly blended.

Have a baking sheet ready and form the tiny meatballs, placing them on the baking sheet as you form them. Italian wedding soup traditionally uses meatballs small enough to get approximately 70 out of the above ingredients. You may make the larger if desired, and adjust the cooking time accordingly.

Place the baking sheet in the oven and bake for approximately 15-20, or until they are evenly browned, turning once halfway through.

Remove the meatballs from the oven and set aside.

In a large stockpot, add the chicken or beef stock, red wine, onion, carrots, bay leaves and rosemary. Bring to a boil and add the meatballs.
Reduce to simmer and let cook 30 minutes for flavors to blend.
Add the spinach and lemon juice. Cook for 10 more minutes. Serve warm.

Rich and Savory Minestrone

Prep Time: 10 minutes

Cook Time: 40 minutes

Servings: 6

Calories: 278

Fat: 13g

Protein: 13g

Net carbs: 18g

Ingredients:

¼ cup olive oil

1 cup red onion, diced

4 cloves garlic, crushed and minced

1 cup carrot, diced

1 cup zucchini, halved and sliced

½ cup celery diced

2 cups tomatoes, chopped

8 cups chicken stock

1 cup spicy tomato juice

1 15 ounce can kidney beans, rinsed and drained

5 cups fresh spinach, torn

½ cup fresh basil, chopped

½ cup fresh parsley, chopped

1 sprig rosemary

2 bay leaves

1 teaspoon salt

2 teaspoons ground black pepper

Fresh parmesan for garnish, if desired

Directions:

In a large stockpot add the olive oil and heat over medium. Add the onion and garlic. Sauté until just soft, approximately 3 minutes.

Add the carrot, zucchini and celery. Cook, stirring often for 5 minutes.

Add the tomatoes, chicken stock, tomato juice, cannellini beans, and kidney beans. Stir well, bring to boil before reducing to a simmer and cook for 5 minutes.

Add the spinach and season with the basil, parsley, rosemary, bay leaves, salt and pepper. Cover and allow to cook for 30 minutes. Serve warm, garnished with fresh parmesan, if desired.

Toscana Soup

Prep Time: 10 minutes

Cook Time: 50 minutes

Servings: 6

Calories: 474

Fat: 33g

Protein: 20g

Net carbs: 16g

Ingredients:

1 lb. ground Italian sausage

1 cup yellow onion, diced

4 cloves garlic, crushed and minced

2 cups acorn squash, cubed

3 cups kale, chopped

½ cup dry white wine

6 cups chicken stock

1 cup heavy cream

2 teaspoons oregano

1 tablespoon fresh rosemary

½ cup fresh basil

1 teaspoon salt

1 teaspoon white pepper

Chopped bacon for garnish, if desired

Directions:

In a large stockpot, brown the Italian sausage over medium heat. Add the onion and garlic, sautéing until just soft, approximately 3 minutes.

Add the acorn squash, kale and white wine. Cook for 5 minutes, while stirring frequently.

Add in the chicken stock and heavy cream. Bring to a boil and then reduce to a simmer. Season with oregano, rosemary, basil, salt and white pepper.

Cover and cook for 40 minutes. Serve warm. Garnish with chopped bacon, of desired.

Rustic Cioppino

Prep Time: 10 minutes

Cook Time: 50 minutes

Servings: 6

Calories: 503

Fat: 15g

Protein: 65g

Net carbs: 17g

Ingredients:

3 tablespoons olive oil

1 cup yellow onion, diced

½ cup fennel, sliced

3 cloves garlic, crushed and minced

1 cup dry white wine

1 cup clam juice

4 cups vegetable or fish stock

¼ cup tomato paste

1 28 ounce can diced tomatoes, including liquid

1 lb. medium shrimp, cleaned and deveined

1 lb. salmon fillet, cubed

1 lb. mussels

1 lb. clams

1 teaspoon crushed red pepper flakes

2 bay leaves

¼ cup fresh basil

1 teaspoon ground black peppercorns

1 teaspoon salt

Directions:

In a large stockpot heat olive oil over medium. Add onion, fennel and garlic. Sauté until just soft, approximately 5 minutes.

Add the white wine and let it reduce while stirring for approximately 3 minutes.

Add the clam juice, vegetable or fish stock, tomato paste and diced tomatoes. Stir well.

Season with crushed red pepper, bay leaves, basil, peppercorns and salt. Bring to a boil while stirring.

Cover and reduce heat to a simmer, cooking for 20-25 minutes. Remove the lid and add the clams and mussels. Cover and cook 5-7 minutes, or until mussels begin to steam open.

Add the shrimp and salmon. Cover and cook for 10-15 minutes, or until shrimp and salmon are cooked through.
Serve warm.

Zucchini Noodle Salad

Prep Time: 15 minutes

Cook Time: 5 minutes +2 hours chilling

Servings: 4

Calories: 354

Fat: 26g

Protein: 14g

Net carbs: 10g

Ingredients:

5 medium zucchini, ends trimmed

1 teaspoon vegetable oil

3 cups fresh basil, firmly packed

½ cup fresh mint

½ cup fresh parsley

3 cloves garlic, crushed and minced

½ cup olive oil

3 tablespoons lemon juice

½ cup fresh grated parmesan cheese

1 teaspoon salt

1 teaspoon pepper

20 cherry tomatoes, cut in half

2 cups broccoli florets

1 medium yellow pepper, sliced

1 cup fresh mozzarella, cubed

Directions:

Thinly julienne the zucchini so that it resembles the thickness of cooked linguine noodles.

In a sauté pan heat the vegetable oil over medium heat. Add the zucchini and sauté until just slightly tender, approximately 3 minutes. Do not overcook. Transfer to a bowl and set aside.

In a blender or food processor, blend the basil, mint, parsley, garlic, olive oil, lemon juice, parmesan cheese, salt and pepper. Blend until creamy.

Add sauce to zucchini and toss to coat.

Add the tomatoes, broccoli, yellow pepper
and mozzarella. Toss gently to mix.
Cover and refrigerate for two hours
before serving.

Italian Chop Salad

Prep Time: 15 minutes+chilling time

Cook Time: 0 minutes

Servings: 4-6

Calories: 443

Fat: 35g

Protein: 13g

Net carbs: 16g

Ingredients:

4 cups romaine lettuce, chopped

1 small head red cabbage, chopped

1 cup cooked garbanzo beans

1 cup cooked bacon, crumbled

1 medium cucumber, chopped

1 cup tomato, diced

¼ cup green onions, sliced

½ cup walnuts, chopped

1 cup gorgonzola cheese, crumbled

½ cup olive oil

½ cup red wine vinegar

1 tablespoon honey

1 tablespoon Dijon mustard

3 cloves garlic, crushed and minced

½ teaspoon oregano

½ teaspoon thyme

½ teaspoon onion powder

2 tablespoons fresh grated parmesan cheese

½ teaspoon salt

1 teaspoon white pepper

Directions:

In a large bowl combine the romaine lettuce, red cabbage and garbanzo beans. Toss to mix well.

In a separate bowl, combine the olive oil, red wine vinegar, honey, Dijon mustard, garlic, oregano, thyme, onion powder,

parmesan cheese, salt and white pepper.
Whisk well until slightly emulsified.

Drizzle the dressing over the salad and
toss to coat.
Add the bacon, cucumber, tomato, green
onions, walnuts and gorgonzola cheese.
Toss to mix.

Cover and refrigerate 1-2 hours. Toss
slightly before serving.

Italian Chicken Salad

Prep Time: 15 minutes

Cook Time: 0 minutes

Servings: 4

Calories: 275

Fat: 15g

Protein: 22g

Net carbs: 10g

Ingredients:

¼ cup olive oil

¼ cup red wine vinegar

1 tablespoon lemon juice

1 clove garlic, crushed and minced

1 teaspoon lemon zest

1 teaspoon rosemary

½ teaspoon salt

1 teaspoon black pepper

3 cups cooked boneless, skinless chicken breast, cubed

1 small red onion, thinly slice

1 cup red bell pepper, finely chopped

20 large black olives, quartered

1 tablespoon capers

1 cup canned artichoke hearts, drained and chopped

¼ cup fresh Italian parsley

Shaved parmesan, for garnish

Directions:

In a bowl combine the olive oil, red wine vinegar, lemon juice, garlic, lemon zest, rosemary, salt and pepper. Whisk until well blended and slightly emulsified. Set aside.

In a large bowl combine the chicken, red onion, red bell pepper, olives, capers, artichoke hearts and parsley.

Drizzle with the prepared dressing and toss well to coat.

Let chill for one hour, if desired.

Garnish with shaved parmesan before serving.

Best Ever Antipasto Salad

Prep Time: 15 minutes+ chilling

Cook Time: 0 minutes

Servings: 6

Calories: 408

Fat: 26g

Protein: 26g

Net carbs: 11g

Ingredients:

½ lb. sopressata salami, cubed

½ lb. smoked Italian ham, cubed

½ cup roasted red peppers

1 cup assorted olives, halved

20 cherry tomatoes, halved

1 cup cucumber, halved and sliced

½ cup marinated artichoke hearts, chopped

1 cup cooked lima beans

1 cup mini fresh mozzarella pearls

2 tablespoons olive oil

2 tablespoons balsamic or red wine
vinegar

2 cloves garlic, crushed and minced

½ cup fresh basil

1 teaspoon coarse ground black pepper

Directions:

In a large bowl combine the sopressata,
smoked Italian ham, roasted red peppers
and olives. Toss to mix.

Add in the tomatoes, cucumber, artichoke
hearts, lima beans and mozzarella pearls.
Mix well.

Drizzle with olive oil and vinegar. Season
with garlic, basil and black pepper. Toss
to mix.

Cover and refrigerate for two hours before serving.

Main Dish Events

When you think of the perfect Italian main dish, it likely is heavily accompanied by mounds of pasta and sauces with just a bit too much sugar to balance the acidity. This is more of our own perception of Italian cuisine. True Italian main dishes highlight the flavors of the ingredients to perfection and tend to not hide them within a portion of pasta. It is entirely possible to savor all of the flavors of the region without blowing your weekly allowance of carbohydrates. In many of the recipes that follow, carb loaded ingredients have been replaced with fresh vegetables, best when prepared at their peak of ripeness, just like in the mother country.

Zucchini Lasagna

Prep Time: 15 minutes

Cook Time: 40 minutes

Servings: 8

Calories: 200

Fat: 12g

Protein: 14g

Net carbs: 8g

Ingredients:

2-3 medium zucchini, sliced lengthwise

½ lb. ground Italian sausage

½ cup onion, chopped

½ cup tomatoes, diced

½ cup carrots, diced

2 cups mushrooms, sliced

1 6 ounce can tomato paste

3 cloves garlic, crushed and minced

¼ cup fresh basil

1 teaspoon oregano

½ teaspoon thyme

1 teaspoon black pepper

½ teaspoon salt

1 egg, beaten

1 cup low fat ricotta cheese

1 cup fresh mozzarella cheese, shredded

Directions:

Preheat oven to 375 degrees Fahrenheit. Bring salted water to boil in a medium saucepan. Place zucchini in water and cook until just tender. Drain and set aside.

In a pan over medium heat, brown the ground sausage removing any excess grease or fat at the end.

To the sausage add the onion, tomatoes, carrots and mushrooms. Cooke for 5-7 minutes over medium heat.

Add the tomato paste, garlic, basil, oregano, thyme, black pepper and salt. Mix well while cooking for an additional minute. Remove from heat and set aside. In a bowl combine the egg, ricotta and mozzarella cheese. Mix well. Lightly oil a 9x13 inch baking pan.

Place a layer of meat mixture, topped with slices of zucchini in the pan. Top with one half of the ricotta mixture. Repeat the layers using the remaining ingredients.

Place in the oven and bake for 30-35 minutes. Let sit 5 minutes before serving.

Meatballs Parmesan

Prep Time: 15 minutes

Cook Time: 35 minutes

Servings: 6

Calories: 490

Fat: 36g

Protein: 35g

Net carbs: 5g

Ingredients:

1 ½ lb. ground beef

1 cup fresh grated parmesan cheese

2 eggs

¼ cup fresh basil, finely chopped

¼ cup fresh parsley, finely chopped

3 cloves garlic, crushed and minced

¼ cup yellow onion, finely diced

½ teaspoon oregano

½ teaspoon salt

½ teaspoon pepper

1 cup prepared, low sugar marinara sauce

½ cup fresh mozzarella cheese, grated

½ cup provolone cheese, grated

Fresh garden greens as a side

Directions:

Preheat oven to 350 degrees Fahrenheit.
In a bowl combine the ground beef,
parmesan cheese and eggs. Mix well with
your hands until meat mixture is moist.

Add in the basil, parsley. Garlic, onion and oregano. Season with salt and pepper as desired. Mix until all ingredients are well incorporated.

Form meat into 1 ½ - 2 inch meatballs. Place on a baking sheet and bake in the oven for 20-25 minutes, or until cooked through.

Place meatballs in a baking dish and cover with marinara sauce. Top the meatballs with fresh mozzarella and provolone cheese. Place back in the oven and cook until sauce is heated through and cheese is melted, approximately 15 minutes.

Remove from the oven and serve with a generous portion of fresh salad greens.

Taste of Italy Casserole

Prep Time: 15 minutes

Cook Time: 40 minutes

Servings: 6

Calories: 397

Fat: 27g

Protein: 31g

Net carbs: 7g

Ingredients:

1 lb. Italian sausage, casing removed

3 cups fresh spinach, torn

2 cups fresh mushroom mixture, sliced

½ cup red onion, diced

3 cloves garlic, crushed and minced

2 cups fresh mozzarella cheese, shredded

1 cup low fat cottage cheese

1 egg

1 teaspoon oregano

½ teaspoon thyme

¼ cup fresh basil, chopped

1 ½ cup fresh tomatoes, chopped

½ cup fresh grated parmesan cheese

Directions:

Preheat oven to 350 degrees Fahrenheit. Over medium heat, brown the Italian sausage. Remove from pan leaving a small amount of the resulting grease in the pan.

Add the spinach, mushroom, onions and garlic to the pan. Sauté just until onions and garlic begin to become translucent. Add the sausage back into the pan and keep warm over low heat.

In a bowl combine the mozzarella cheese, cottage cheese, egg, oregano, thyme and basil.

Spoon ½ of the sausage mixture into a 9x9 inch baking dish. Add a layer of half of the cottage cheese mixture over the sausage. Repeat for a second layer of each.

Top the casserole with chopped tomatoes and fresh grated parmesan cheese. Place in the oven and bake for 25-30 minutes. Let rest 5 minutes before serving.

.

Eggplant Manicotti

Prep Time: 20 minutes

Cook Time: 1 hour

Servings: 6-8

Calories: 260

Fat: 12g

Protein: 18g

Net carbs: 16g

Ingredients:

2 tablespoons olive oil

1 cup yellow onion, diced

5 cloves garlic, crushed and minced

¼ cup red wine

1 28 ounce can crushed tomatoes

1 cup beef stock

1 tablespoon balsamic vinegar

1 teaspoon rosemary

1 teaspoon oregano

¼ cup fresh basil, chopped

2 medium sized eggplants, sliced lengthwise into ¼ inch thickness

1 cup cottage cheese

1 cup low fat ricotta cheese, excess liquid strained

½ cup fresh grated parmesan cheese

1 egg, beaten

¼ cup fresh chives, chopped

1 ½ cup fresh spinach, chopped

½ cup onion, diced

1 teaspoon nutmeg

1 teaspoon salt

1 teaspoon coarse ground black pepper

Fresh basil to garnish

Directions:

Begin by preparing the sauce for the manicotti. Heat the olive oil in a sauté pan over medium heat. Add the onion and garlic and cook until onion begins to soften, approximately 3 minutes.

Add the red wine and balsamic vinegar, continue cooking to reduce the sauce for approximately 3-5 minutes.

Add the tomatoes and beef stock. Season with the rosemary, oregano and basil. Bring to a boil, and then reduce heat to a simmer. Cover and cook for 20-25 minutes.

Remove from heat and set aside. Preheat oven to 350 degrees Fahrenheit.

In a bowl combine the cottage cheese, ricotta cheese, parmesan cheese and egg. Mix until smooth.

Add the chives, spinach and onion. Season with nutmeg, salt and pepper. On a lightly oiled baking sheet place the eggplant slices and season them with salt and pepper, if desired.

Place the baking sheet in the oven and cook until the eggplant slices are tender enough to be rolled, approximately 10-15 minutes. Remove from the oven and set aside.

Add equal amounts of the cheese mixture down the center of each slice of eggplant. Roll each piece up and place seam side down in a 9x13 inch baking dish.

Cover eggplant manicotti with sauce, tapping gently to make sure the sauce is distributed along the bottom of the baking dish as well as the top.
Place in the oven and bake for 25-30 minutes.

Let sit 10 minutes before serving. Garnish with fresh basil, if desired.

Italian Seaside Boil

Prep Time: 10 minutes

Cook Time: 20-25 minutes

Servings: 8

Calories: 447

Fat: 12g

Protein: 61g

Net carbs: 15g

Ingredients:

2 tablespoons olive oil

4 cloves garlic, crushed and minced

½ cup onion, diced

1 medium sized fennel bulb, chopped

1 28 ounce can crushed tomatoes, with liquid

1 medium tomato, diced

3 tablespoons tomato paste

1 cup dry white wine

4 cups fish stock or vegetable stock

2 bay leaves

1 tablespoon old bay seasoning

1 lb. mussels

½ lb. scallops

1 lb. shrimp, cleaned and deveined

1 lb. salmon, cubed

2 fresh corn cons, cut into quarters

1 medium red pepper, cubed

Directions:

Heat the olive oil in a stockpot over medium heat. Add the garlic, onion and fennel. Cook, tossing gently, until the fennel begins to become tender and slightly translucent, approximately 5 minutes.

Add the canned tomatoes with liquid, diced tomatoes and tomato paste. Stir gently.

Add the white wine and fish or vegetable stock. Season with the bay leaves and old bay seasoning. Bring the mixture to a boil. Cover and reduce heat to low. Let simmer for 15 minutes.

Add the corn cobs and red bell pepper to the broth.

Add the mussels and scallops. Cook for two minutes before adding the salmon and shrimp. Cook until seafood is tenderly cooked through, taking care not to overcook. Serve immediately.

Forget the Noodles Shrimp Scampi

Prep Time: 5 minutes

Cook Time: 15 minutes

Servings: 4

Calories: 262

Fat: 13g

Protein: 27g

Net carbs: 5g

Ingredients:

3 tablespoons unsalted butter

4 cloves garlic, crushed and minced

1 small jalapeno pepper, finely diced

1 lb. medium shrimp, cleaned and deveined

¼ cup dry white wine

¼ cup fish stock or chicken stock

¼ cup fresh parsley, chopped

¼ cup fresh basil, chopped

2 tablespoons fresh lemon juice

1 teaspoon lemon zest

3 cups zucchini, julienned lengthwise

¼ cup fresh grated parmesan cheese

1 teaspoon salt

1 teaspoon pepper

Directions:

Melt the butter in a large sauté pan over medium heat. Add garlic and jalapeno. Sauté until just fragrant, approximately 2 minutes.

Add the shrimp and cook while tossing gently for 3 minutes.

Add the white wine and fish stock. Season with parsley, basil, lemon juice and lemon zest. Stir to blend flavors.

Add the zucchini and cook until just tender, approximately 5 minutes. Serve immediately. Garnish with fresh parmesan cheese and season with salt and pepper.

Spaghetti Squash Alfredo

Prep Time: 10 minutes

Cook Time: 45 minutes

Servings: 4

Calories: 577

Fat: 51g

Protein: 19g

Net carbs: 10g

Ingredients:

1 medium sized spaghetti squash, cut in half

1 tablespoon olive oil

¼ cup butter

1 cup heavy cream

3 cloves garlic, crushed and minced

1 shallot, finely diced

1 cup fresh grated parmesan cheese

½ cup grated asiago cheese

1 teaspoon basil

1 teaspoon oregano

1 teaspoon salt

1 teaspoon pepper

Directions:

Preheat oven to 350 degrees.

Remove seeds from the spaghetti squash halves. Place the halves on a baking sheet and brush with olive oil. Place in the oven and bake for 30-35 minutes, or until squash becomes tender.

Remove the squash from the oven and allow to cool enough to handle. Scoop out the insides of the squash into a bowl, "fluff" with a fork and set aside.

In a sauté pan over medium heat, melt the butter. Add the garlic and shallot. Sauté until just tender, approximately 2-3 minutes.

Add the heavy cream, parmesan and asiago cheeses. Using a whisk, briskly mix the sauce until all ingredients are well incorporated and heated through. Season with basil, oregano, salt and pepper to taste.

Take the reserved spaghetti squash and add it to the pan. Fluff the squash strands will coating with the sauce. Continue to cook until the squash is heated through.

Remove from heat and serve immediately.

Spaghetti Squash Pizza Pie

Prep Time: 15 minutes

Cook Time: 1 ½ hours

Servings: 6

Calories: 332

Fat: 22g

Protein: 17g

Net carbs: 12g

Ingredients:

1 medium sized spaghetti squash, cut in half

1 teaspoon olive oil

1 lb. Italian sausage, casing removed

1 cup yellow onion, diced

1 cup portabella mushrooms, sliced

½ cup kalmata olives, sliced

1 cup low sugar tomato or pizza sauce

1 cup low fat ricotta cheese

2 eggs, beaten

½ cup fresh chives, chopped

½ cup fresh basil, chopped

1 teaspoon crushed red pepper flakes

1 teaspoon salt

1 teaspoon pepper

Directions:

Preheat oven to 350 degrees Fahrenheit.

Brush the squash halves with olive oil and place them cut side down on a baking sheet. Place the baking sheet in the oven and bake for 30-40 minutes, or until squash is tender.

Remove the squash from the oven and let cool enough to handle. Remove the squash strands and place them in a bowl. "Fluff" lightly with a fork.

In a sauté pan over medium heat, brown the sausage. Add the onion and mushrooms. Sauté until tender, approximately 3 minutes.

Stir in the olives and tomato sauce. Season with basil, crushed red pepper flakes, salt and pepper to taste.

Reduce heat to low and let the sauce simmer for 10-15 minutes. In a small bowl combine the ricotta cheese, eggs and fresh chives. Mix well.

Place the spaghetti squash in a lightly oiled 9x9 baking dish. Add the sauce and mix well, making sure to thoroughly coat the spaghetti squash.

Top with dollops of the ricotta mixture. Place in the oven and bake for 40-45 minutes. Let sit 10 minutes before serving.

Spaghetti Squash "Noodles"

Prep Time: 10 minutes

Cook Time: 40 minutes

Servings: 4

Calories: 138

Fat: 9g

Protein: 6g

Net carbs: 8g

Ingredients:

1 medium sized spaghetti squash

2 teaspoons olive oil

1 teaspoon fresh lemon juice

¼ teaspoon nutmeg

½ teaspoon onion powder

1 tablespoon fresh parsley, chopped

1 tablespoon fresh basil, chopped

½ teaspoon salt

1 teaspoon coarse ground black pepper

½ cup goat cheese, crumbled

Directions:

Preheat oven to 350 degrees Fahrenheit. Cut spaghetti squash in half lengthwise, remove any seeds and brush with olive oil.

Place the squash cut side down on a baking sheet and place in the oven. Bake for 35-40 minutes, or until squash is tender.

Remove squash from oven and scoop the insides into a large serving bowl.
Sprinkle the squash with fresh lemon juice and season with nutmeg, onion powder, parsley, basil, salt and pepper. Toss to coat.

Top with crumbled goat cheese before serving.

Meatza Pie

Prep Time: 10 minutes

Cook Time: 40 minutes

Servings: 8

Calories: 214

Fat: 15g

Protein: 14g

Net carbs: 4g

Ingredients:

1 lb. ground beef

2 cloves garlic, crushed and minced

1 teaspoon crushed red pepper flakes

1 teaspoon rosemary

1 teaspoon thyme

½ teaspoon salt

1 teaspoon pepper

½ cup low sugar tomato or pizza sauce

¼ cup sundried tomatoes, chopped

½ cup artichoke hearts, chopped

½ cup red onion, thinly sliced

1 cup portabella mushrooms, sliced

½ cup fresh mozzarella

½ cup arugula leaves

1 teaspoon olive oil

¼ cup fresh basil, torn

Directions:

Preheat oven to 400 degrees Fahrenheit.

In a bowl combine the ground beef with the garlic, crushed red pepper, rosemary, thyme, salt and pepper. Mix well.

Press the meat mixture into the bottom of a 9x13 baking pan. Place in the oven and bake until meat crust is cooked through, approximately 15 minutes.

Remove the meat crust from the oven. Top the meat with the tomato sauce, sundried tomatoes, artichoke hearts, red onion and portabella mushrooms.

Add the fresh mozzarella and place back in the oven for 10 minutes, or until cheese is bubbly and slightly golden in color.

Garnish with fresh arugula, olive oil and basil before serving.

Mama's Italian Meatloaf

Prep Time: 15 minutes

Cook Time: 1 hour

Servings: 6-8

Calories: 542

Fat: 40g

Protein: 36g

Net carbs: 5g

Ingredients:

2 lbs. ground beef

½ lb. ground pork sausage

2 tablespoons balsamic vinegar

2 tablespoons Worcestershire sauce

3 eggs

1 cup red onion, finely diced

3 cloves garlic, crushed and minced

½ cup olives (any variety), finely chopped

½ cup red bell pepper, diced

½ cup fresh basil, chopped

1 tablespoon fresh parsley, chopped

1 cup grated parmesan cheese

1 cup low sugar tomato or marinara sauce

½ cup grated asiago cheese

Directions:

Preheat oven to 350 degrees Fahrenheit.

In a bowl, combine the ground beef, pork sausage, balsamic vinegar,

Worcestershire sauce and eggs. Mix with your hands and well blended and moistened.

Mix in the red onion, garlic, olives, red bell pepper, basil, parsley and parmesan cheese.

Place the meat mixture into a lightly oiled loaf pan. Top with tomato or marinara sauce and place in the oven. Bake for 40 minutes.

Add the asiago cheese onto the top of the meatloaf and place back in the oven for 10-15 additional minutes, or until meatloaf is cooked all the way through. Let sit 10 minutes before serving.

Slow Cooker Chicken Cacciatore

Prep Time: 10 minutes

Cook Time: 6 hours

Servings: 8

Calories: 218

Fat: 4g

Protein: 28g

Net carbs: 7g

Ingredients:

2 lbs. boneless, skinless chicken pieces

1 cup green bell pepper, chopped

1 cup button mushrooms, sliced

1 cup red onion, thinly sliced

4 cloves garlic, crushed and minced

½ cup tomato paste

1 cup chicken broth

½ cup dry red wine

1 teaspoon oregano

1 teaspoon thyme

1 teaspoon rosemary

1 teaspoon salt

1teaspoon black pepper

Directions:

Place the chicken in a slow cooker. Add the green bell pepper, mushrooms and onion.

In a small bowl combine the garlic, tomato paste, chicken broth and red wine. Mix well.

Pour the mixture over the chicken and vegetables. Season with oregano, thyme, rosemary, salt and pepper.

Cook on low for six hours. Serve warm with fresh greens.

Parmesan Crusted Chicken with Mushrooms

Prep Time: 15 minutes

Cook Time: 40 minutes

Servings: 6

Calories: 273

Fat: 12g

Protein: 36g

Net carbs: 2g

Ingredients:

2 lbs. boneless skinless chicken breast

¼ cup mayonnaise

¼ cup fresh grated parmesan

¼ cup fresh parsley, chopped

¼ cup fresh chives, chopped

1 teaspoon salt

1 teaspoon pepper

1 cup portabella mushrooms, sliced

½ cup red onion, thinly sliced

1 tablespoon olive oil

¼ cup dry white wine

Directions:

Preheat the oven to 400 degrees Fahrenheit. Lightly oil a 9x9 or larger baking pan.

In a bowl combine the parmesan cheese, parsley, chives, salt and pepper. Brush each piece of chicken with mayonnaise and then pat well with the parmesan mixture to coat.

Place chicken in the baking dish and bake in the oven for 30-35 minutes or until chicken juices run clear.

Approximately ten minutes before the chicken is done baking add the olive oil to a sauté pan. Sauté the mushrooms and

onion until tender, approximately 3-5
minutes.

Add the white wine and continue cooking
for 3 minutes while the wine reduces.
Remove the chicken from the oven and let
rest 5 minutes before serving. Serve
topped with sautéed mushrooms.

Stuffed Chicken Italiano

Prep Time: 15 minutes

Cook Time: 50 minutes

Servings: 4

Calories: 450

Fat: 11g

Protein: 56g

Net carbs: 4g

Ingredients:

4 boneless, skinless chicken breasts

2 cups fresh spinach, torn

¼ cup sundried tomatoes, chopped

½ cup red onion, diced

2 cloves garlic, crushed and minced

1 cup fresh mozzarella cheese

1 teaspoon nutmeg

1 teaspoon salt

1 teaspoon pepper

1 cup chicken stock

1 tablespoon olive oil

Directions:

Preheat oven to 350 degrees Fahrenheit. Heat some olive oil in a sauté pan over medium heat. Add the onion and garlic. Sauté until tender, approximately 3-5 minutes.

Add the spinach and tomatoes. Continue cooking until spinach wilts, approximately 3 minutes. Season with nutmeg, salt and pepper. Remove from heat and set aside.

Take each piece of chicken and make a cut lengthwise along the side of each breast, taking care to not cut all of the way through. Take the spinach mixture and stuff equal amounts into the cut of each chicken breast.

Next stuff equal portions of fresh mozzarella cheese into each breast. Pour the chicken stock into a baking dish. Place the chicken into the baking dish. Brush with additional olive oil and seasonings, if desired.

Place in the oven and cook for 40-45 minutes or until chicken juices run clear.

Lazy Day Easy Artichoke Chicken

Prep Time: 10 minutes

Cook Time: 6 hours

Servings: 4

Calories: 417

Fat: 7g

Protein: 56g

Net carbs: 18g

Ingredients:

4 boneless, skinless chicken breasts

1 14 ounce can crushed tomatoes, with liquid

1 cup artichoke hearts, coarsely chopped

1 cup red onion, sliced

3 cloves garlic, crushed and minced

1 medium red bell pepper, sliced

1 cup chicken broth

½ cup dry white wine

1 teaspoon oregano

¼ cup fresh parsley, chopped

1 teaspoon thyme

1 teaspoon salt

1 teaspoon pepper

¼ cup fresh basil, chopped

Directions:

Place chicken, tomatoes with liquid, artichoke hearts, red onion, garlic and red bell pepper in a slow cooker.

In a separate bowl combine the chicken broth, white wine, oregano, parsley, thyme, salt and pepper. Mix well and pour over the chicken.

Cook on low for 6 hours, or until chicken juices run clear. Garnish with fresh basil before serving.

Traditional Stuffed Bell Peppers

Prep Time: 10 minutes

Cook Time: 40 minutes

Servings: 4

Calories: 382

Fat: 25g

Protein: 23g

Net carbs: 9g

Ingredients:

4 green peppers, tops and seeds removed

1 tablespoon extra virgin olive oil

½ cup yellow onion, diced

3 cloves garlic, crushed and minced

1 cup portabella mushrooms, sliced

¼ cup dry red wine

½ lb. Italian sausage, casings removed

1 ½ cup canned crushed tomatoes, including liquid

½ cup fresh grated parmesan cheese

¼ fresh parsley, chopped

¼ cup fresh basil, chopped

1 teaspoon oregano

1 teaspoon thyme

1 teaspoon onion powder

1 teaspoon salt

1 teaspoon pepper

½ cup fresh mozzarella cheese, shredded

Directions:

Preheat oven to 375 degrees Fahrenheit. Heat the olive oil in a sauté pan over medium heat. Sauté the onion and garlic until tender, approximately 3 minutes. Add the mushrooms and cook for an additional minute.

Add the red wine and cook for 2 minutes while the wine reduces. Add the Italian sausage and cook until browned.

Add the crushed tomatoes, parmesan cheese, parsley, basil, oregano, thyme, onion powder, salt and pepper. Stir well and cook until warmed through. Remove from heat and set aside.

Place the bell peppers, cut side up, in a baking dish. Stuff each pepper with equal amounts of the sausage mixture. Top each pepper with the mozzarella cheese.

Place in the oven and bake for 20-25 minutes, or until cheese is golden colored and pepper is slightly tender.

Conclusion

Italian cuisine nourishes both the body and the spirit. For far too long many of us have lived without the nourishing comfort of Italian favorites. Our diets and health have dictated that we pay closer attention to the foods that we consume and how we take care of our bodies. This is very important for the long term health of each person. As someone that has made a commitment to live a low carb lifestyle, you understand probably better than most what it means to adjust the foods that you eat and enjoy in order to maintain your diet. Italian food is one of the cuisines of the world that fits wonderfully into a low carb lifestyle. This is contrary to what many of us believe. The truth is that true Italian flavors are naturally low in carbohydrates, It is usually what accompanies these flavors, such as pastas, that are detrimental to the healthiness of the dish.

Within this book we have made a point in showing you just how Italian flavors can be showcased in a low carbohydrate manner at your dinner table. We have included everything from light soups, nourishing salads to fully rich and flavorful main dishes. You will find that you are not missing a single thing, and in fact you may notice how the traditional flavors of Italy are highlighted once you remove the not so healthy elements that us in the western world have added in to this otherwise healthy style of food. I hope that you have enjoyed taking a look at all of the wonderful ways in which you can bring Italian favorites back to your table. Each should be crafted with love and shared with those closest to your heart, just like in the land where they originated.

Made in the USA
San Bernardino, CA
19 February 2016